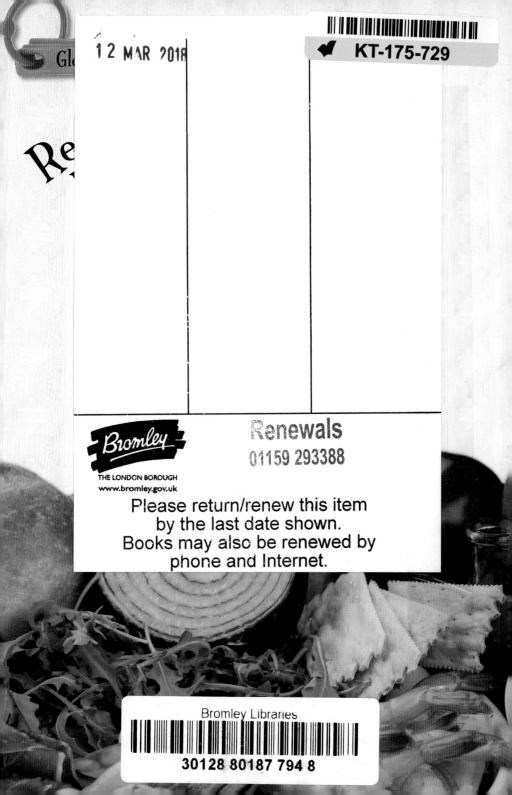

Raintree is an imprint of Capstone Global Library Limited, a company incorporated in England and Wales having its registered office at 7 Pilgrim Street, London, EC4V 6LB – Registered company number: 6695582

www.raintreepublishers.co.uk
myorders@raintreepublishers.co.uk

Edited by Abby Colich, Laura Knowles, and John-Paul Wilkins
Designed by Cynthia Akiyoshi
Picture research by Tracy Cummins
Production by Vicki Fitzgerald
Originated by Capstone Global Library
Printed and bound in China

ISBN 978 1 406 27381 6 (hardback)
17 16 15 14 13
10 9 8 7 6 5 4 3 2 1

ISBN 978 1 406 27386 1 (paperback)
18 17 16 15 14
10 9 8 7 6 5 4 3 2 1

A full catalogue record for this book is available from the British Library.

Acknowledgments

We would like to thank the following for permission to reproduce photographs: Capstone Publishers pp. 1, 9–11, 16–43 (Karon Dubke); © Crown p.12 (copyright material is reproduced with the permission of HMSO and Queen's Printer for Scotland, food.gov.uk); Getty Images pp. 7 (Adrian Weinbrecht), 13 (JGI/Jamie Grill), 14 (Lew Robertson), 15 (Henglein and Steets); Shutterstock pp. 4 (Emi Cristea), 5 (Manamana), 6 (Tupungato).

Design elements reproduced with permission of Shutterstock (Alex Studio, Andrey Savin, Angel Simon, anistidesign, Arkady Mazor, Brooke Becker, Christian Jung, draconus, Fedorov Oleksiy, giorgiomtb, IngridsI, Luis Santos, marchello74, Mazzzur, Nordling, oksana2010, photastic, Piccia Neri, Picsfive, Richard Peterson, rook76, Sandra Cunningham, Tim Ackroyd, Tobik, ULKASTUDIO, Viktar Malyshchyts, Volosina).

Cover photograph of a pizza margherita reproduced with permission of Capstone Publishers (Karon Dubke).

We would like to thank Ruth Ben-Ghiat, Sarah Schenker, and Marla Conn for their invaluable help in the preparation of this book.

Disclaimer

Contents

Ancient and modern

Italy is easy to find on a map. At the base of the continent of Europe, Italy looks like a boot dipping its toe into the Mediterranean Sea.

The land varies throughout the country. Skiers enjoy the mountainous Alps on the northern border. Holidaymakers enjoy the coast of the Italian Riviera. In the south, an active volcano, Mount Etna, looms over the island of Sicily.

The Tuscan countryside is bathed in sunshine for much of the year.

Throughout its long history, Italy has been a centre of art and culture. Thousands of years ago, Rome, the current capital of Italy, ruled the Roman Empire. This empire stretched west into Europe, north into Britain, east into Asia, and south into parts of Africa. Over water and land, Rome traded new goods and traditions with its conquered regions. Rome influenced the art, science, and literature of the known world.

Today, Italy has a diverse community. The north contains more cities, while the south has more farmers. Like many modern cities around the world, Italian cities are filled with large apartment and business buildings. In older sections, however, you can still see the narrow streets and piazzas, or city squares, from long ago. In the countryside, towns and villages are filled with people who have close ties to their families and communities.

Italy is a modern country that still holds memories of its past. Children pass the ruins of the Colosseum on their way to school. Friends play football on a field that was once a chariot racetrack. People may take a lunch break sitting at the base of an ancient marble statue. The richness of Italy's past is still a part of Italian life today.

A network of canals weaves its way through the beautiful city of Venice. Tourists flock to the city from all over the world.

Buon appetito

Pasta and pizza may be the first things to come to mind when you think of Italian food. But they are only a small part of it. Italy's many regions have developed their own special dishes. In areas near the coast, seafood is an important part of many meals. Rice grows best in the Po Basin of northern Italy. Almond trees thrive in the heat of the south. Even specific cities and towns are known for certain foods, such as prosciutto ham in Parma, grilled steak in Florence, and risotto in Milan. Northern Italian meals are known to include rice, butter, and cream. Southern Italian dishes often contain olive oil, tomato, and pasta.

Come rain or shine, Italians visit outdoor markets for a selection of fresh ingredients.

Italian meals

An Italian's day starts out with a quick breakfast. Lunch is the largest meal. In many towns, shops and businesses close from noon until around 4.00 p.m. so that people can enjoy this meal at home. Dinner is a much lighter meal eaten later in the evening.

Food and family go hand in hand in Italy. Mealtimes are a chance to relax and enjoy some quality time together.

Traditionally, a large Italian meal has many courses. *Antipasto* means "before the meal" and often includes small pieces of cured meats and cheeses. The *primo piatto* (first course) is a small plate of pasta or risotto, or a bowl of soup. The *secondo piatto* (second course) is a meat or fish dish. Finally, *dolce* (dessert) is often fresh fruit or another sweet creation.

Before Italians begin to eat, they may wish for a good meal for everyone – *Buon appetito!*

Italian ingredients

Here are some ingredients found in Italian households and in the recipes in this book. If you can't find a certain ingredient, look for similar replacements.

Olives and olive oil give many Italian dishes their distinctive flavour. Olives are preserved in brine. Olive oil comes from olives that are pressed. Extra-virgin is the best.

Balsamic vinegar is a thick, brown vinegar with a rich and slightly sweet flavour.

Cheeses are made mostly from cow's milk in the north, and goat's and sheep's milk in the south. Some common Italian cheeses include Parmigiano-Reggiano (Parmesan), mozzarella, and gorgonzola.

Cured meats are preserved, sliced, and used for antipasti (the first course) and other dishes. Recipes in this book use prosciutto, capocollo, mortadella, and pancetta (Italian bacon).

Vegetables are piled high at Italian markets. During the right season, you'll find artichokes, aubergines, mushrooms, peas, tomatoes, carrots, celery, red peppers, and courgettes. Italians also use lots of greens, such as rocket, radicchio, and spinach. Many dishes are seasoned with onion and garlic. Some vegetables, such as artichokes, aubergines, pepperoncini, and red peppers, are marinated in oil and vinegar and kept in jars.

Fruits are often eaten as dessert in Italy. Popular fruits include blood oranges, pears, lemons, melons, plums, pomegranates, strawberries, and figs.

Herbs and spices, such as basil, parsley, thyme, sage, rosemary, hot red pepper flakes, and anise, flavour many Italian dishes.

Nuts help add texture to desserts. Commonly used nuts include almonds, pistachios, pine nuts, hazelnuts, and walnuts.

Pasta comes in hundreds of types – long strings, short tubes, and many other shapes. Many Italians make their pasta fresh, but they also use dry pasta. Many varieties of pasta, both dry and fresh, can be found in supermarkets.

Cornmeal is used to make polenta, a dish in northern Italy that often replaces pasta or bread with a meal. It can be cooked like porridge or grilled like a patty.

Arborio rice is short-grain rice from northern Italy used to make a creamy dish called risotto.

Meat is the basis of the second course of an Italian meal. Veal, lamb, beef, pork, chicken, and rabbit are popular choices.

Beans are a source of protein for Italians. They use cannellini beans, chickpeas, and fava beans.

Seafood and shellfish are eaten fresh, such as scampi, mullet, mussels, squid, and sea bass, or packed in oil, such as tuna, sardines, and anchovies.

Eggs are used for baking, but also for omelettes called frittatas.

Bread and breadsticks accompany many meals to help soak up sauces or to top with treats from an antipasto platter.

Italian meals contain a delicious combination of fresh fruits, vegetables, and cheeses.

How to use this book

Each chapter of this book will introduce you to aspects of Italian cooking. But you don't have to read the book from beginning to end. Flip through, find what interests you, and give it a try. You may discover a recipe that becomes your new favourite meal!

If you already do a lot of cooking, you may know your way around the kitchen. But if you've never diced a tomato, sautéed garlic, or whisked up cream, don't worry. Have a look at the glossary on page 44.

Anise biscuits

Biscotti refers to all kinds of Italian biscuits. These biscotti are the crunchy twice-baked kind that many Italians dip in coffee and eat for breakfast. You can dip them in milk or hot chocolate to soften them up. Anise gives them a slight liquorice flavour.

Ingredients	Tools
225 g sugar	Kitchen scales
50 g unsalted butter	Measuring spoons
2 eggs	Electric hand mixer
¼ teaspoon anise extract (or ½ teaspoon of ground star anise)	Large and medium bowls
	Spatula
300 g flour	Baking tray
1 teaspoon baking powder	Greaseproof paper
¼ teaspoon salt	Cooling rack
50 g flaked almonds	Serrated knife

18

Each recipe is set up the same way: Ingredients lists all the ingredients you'll be adding. Tools tells you the various kitchen utensils you will need. Collect the ingredients and tools before you start working so that you have everything nearby when you need it.

Then just follow the Steps. Make sure you read them carefully. Numbers on the photos indicate which step they refer to. Don't worry if your creation isn't perfect when you reach the end. Cooking takes practice and experimentation. Be patient and enjoy the process.

Steps

1. Preheat oven to 180°C.

2. In a large bowl, cream together the sugar, butter, eggs, and anise extract, and beat with an electric mixer until smooth.

3. In a medium bowl, mix together the flour, baking powder, salt, and almonds.

4. Add the dry ingredients to the wet ones. Stir until just combined to make a soft dough. Be careful not to over mix.

5. Line a baking tray with greaseproof paper. Divide the dough in half. Form each half into a log about 20 centimetres long.

6. Bake for about 30 minutes, until golden brown. Allow to cool for about 15 minutes on a cooling rack.

7. With a serrated knife, cut each log into 1-centimetre-thick diagonal slices. Return the biscuits to the baking tray.

8. Bake for about 8 to 10 minutes, until lightly toasted.

Makes about 2 dozen biscuits
Time: 20 minutes prep,
40 minutes to bake

  Ncontains **uts**   **V**egetarian

Quick tip

Greaseproof paper makes your job easier in two ways. It keeps biscuits from sticking to the baking tray as they bake. And it makes cleaning up much easier. You can find greaseproof paper in your local supermarket.

VARIATION

Play around with different flavours in this breakfast biscuit. Try a different kind of extract, such as vanilla or almond. Try different nuts, too, such as pistachios, walnuts, or hazelnuts.

19

If you have to follow a specific diet, or have food allergies, look for the labels on each recipe. These will tell you if a dish is vegan, vegetarian, dairy-free, gluten-free, or if it contains nuts. However, you should check food packaging before use to be sure.

Ncontains **uts**

Dairy free

Gluten free

Vegetarian

Vegan

Look at Quick tips for cooking and kitchen advice, and Variations for swapping out ingredients for others if you would like.

Whenever you are in the kitchen, ask an adult to help or be nearby. You shouldn't use any knife or appliance without an adult's permission and assistance. You can find more ways to be safe while you cook on page 14.

A healthy kitchen

It's fun to head out on a food adventure by trying new tastes from countries beyond your own. But you should also keep your health in mind. The following are the basic food groups. Italians include all of these groups in a meal, or over the course of a day, to get the proper balance of nutrients to grow and be healthy.

Fruits and vegetables

Italians may sip a glass of blood orange juice in the mornings, or top their panna cotta with strawberries. They also include many healthy vegetables in their diets, such as spinach, peas, and red peppers. Both fruits and vegetables can help rreduce the risk of getting certain diseases. They contain nutrients your body needs and fibre to keep your digestive system running smoothly.

Grains

These are foods made from wheat, rice, corn, oats, or other grains. Whole grains that use the entire grain kernel are the healthiest. Refined grains, such as white flour and white rice, do not have as many vitamins and minerals. Pasta, risotto, and polenta are just a few of the Italian foods in this group. Many pastas and breads come in both white and whole grain varieties.

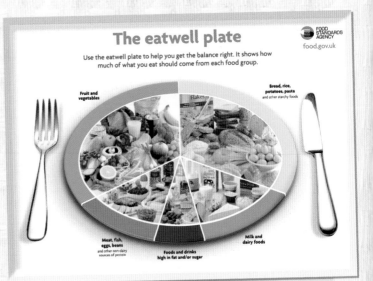

The eatwell plate shows us the importance of eating a combination of all the food groups in our diets.

Italian foods are delicious, and fun to eat, too!

Protein

Protein foods include meats, poultry, seafood, and eggs. It also includes beans (such as cannellini beans used in *pasta e fagioli*) and nuts. Look for low-fat meats. Cured meats, a favourite of Italians, have a lot of added salt. Try to eat these only occasionally.

Dairy

Cheese, ice cream, milk, and any products made from milk fall into this category. Dairy foods contain a lot of bone-building calcium. Hard cheeses, like Parmesan, soft cheeses, like ricotta, and even creamy gelato give Italians a dose of calcium. Choose low-fat options when you can.

Fats and sugar

Some oils, especially the ones from plants, such as olive oil, do provide some important nutrients. Nuts are high in oils, too. But solid fats, such as butter and meat fat, are not as good for you. So use them sparingly. Your body needs sugar, but not too much. Try not to fill up on too many Italian sweets!

A safe kitchen

It can be fun to whip up a tasty new creation in the kitchen, but safety should be your number one concern. Here are some tips to keep in mind:

- Make sure an adult is nearby for permission, help, advice, and assistance.
- Wash your hands before you work.
- Wear the right clothing, including sturdy shoes and an apron.
- Foods can grow harmful bacteria. Make sure you keep foods in the refrigerator or freezer until they are ready to use. Check expiration dates. If something smells or looks funny, it may be spoiled.

It is not just the pan that gets hot when you are boiling water. Be careful of the water and steam, too.

There are lots of delicious meals to try in Italian cooking. But remember to share the fun of cooking with an adult.

- Raw meat, poultry, seafood, and eggs can carry germs. Always wash your hands immediately after touching them. Wash any knife or chopping board after you use them with these foods. Make sure these foods are cooked all the way through before you eat them. Clean worktops and kitchen tools with warm, soapy water when you have finished working.

- On the hob, make sure pan handles point in, so the pans don't get knocked over. Never leave pans unattended. Do not let anything flammable, such as loose sleeves or tea towels, near burners on the hob.

- Always use oven gloves when removing something from the oven or microwave. Avoid steam when you lift a top off a pan on the hob or in the oven.

- Knives are sharp. Always point the blade away from you. Take your time and pay attention to what you are cutting. Don't use a knife without the help of an adult.

Buongiorno! (Good morning!)

For many Italians, a good morning means starting with something sweet. People often stop into pastry shops or coffee bars on their way to work or school. They might get a drink, such as a cappuccino (a foamy mix of coffee and milk) or a glass of blood orange juice, and a pastry or biscuit. They stand at the counter or sit at an outdoor table to enjoy this tasty part of their day.

Cornetti

Cornetti are the Italian version of a French croissant. These flaky pastries are shaped like small horns. They can be plain or filled with cream, fruit, nuts, or chocolate.

Ingredients

- 1 sheet frozen puff pastry dough, thawed
- About 3 tablespoons chocolate hazelnut spread
- 1 egg yolk
- 1 teaspoon milk
- Sugar for sprinkling

Tools

- Rolling pin
- Knife
- Chopping board
- Measuring spoons
- Spreader
- Baking tray
- Small bowl
- Whisk
- Pastry brush

Steps

1. Preheat oven to 220°C.

2. Unfold the puff pastry dough. Roll it with a rolling pin to flatten any seams. Cut the sheet into 4 squares, and then cut each square diagonally into 2 triangles so that you have 8 triangles in all.

3. Place about 1 teaspoon of hazelnut chocolate spread in the centre of each triangle and spread it around. Be careful not to spread right to the edges. Roll up the triangles loosely from one side to the opposite point. Place them on a baking tray.

4. In a small bowl, whisk together the egg yolk and milk. Brush onto each cornetto. Sprinkle them with sugar.

5. Bake for about 12 minutes, or until browned.

Makes 8 cornetti
Time: 15 minutes prep,
12 minutes to bake

 Ncontains **uts**
 Vegetarian

VARIATION

Instead of chocolate hazelnut spread, you can spread any type of fruit jam inside the cornetti, too. Or combine both chocolate hazelnut spread and jam together!

17

Anise biscuits

Biscotti refers to all kinds of Italian biscuits. These biscotti are the crunchy twice-baked kind that many Italians dip in coffee and eat for breakfast. You can dip them in milk or hot chocolate to soften them up. Anise gives them a slight liquorice flavour.

Ingredients	Tools
225 g sugar	Kitchen scales
50 g unsalted butter	Measuring spoons
2 eggs	Electric hand mixer
¼ teaspoon anise extract (or ½ teaspoon of ground star anise)	Large and medium bowls
300 g flour	Spatula
1 teaspoon baking powder	Baking tray
¼ teaspoon salt	Greaseproof paper
50 g flaked almonds	Cooling rack
	Serrated knife

Steps

1. Preheat oven to 180°C.

2. In a large bowl, cream together the sugar, butter, eggs, and anise extract, and beat with an electric mixer until smooth.

3. In a medium bowl, mix together the flour, baking powder, salt, and almonds.

4. Add the dry ingredients to the wet ones. Stir until just combined to make a soft dough. Be careful not to over mix.

5. Line a baking tray with greaseproof paper. Divide the dough in half. Form each half into a log about 20 centimetres long.

6. Bake for about 30 minutes, until golden brown. Allow to cool for about 15 minutes on a cooling rack.

7. With a serrated knife, cut each log into 1-centimetre-thick diagonal slices. Return the biscuits to the baking tray.

8. Bake for about 8 to 10 minutes, until lightly toasted.

Makes about 2 dozen biscuits
Time: 20 minutes prep,
**   40 minutes to bake**

Quick tip

Greaseproof paper makes your job easier in two ways. It keeps biscuits from sticking to the baking tray as they bake. And it makes cleaning up much easier. You can find greaseproof paper in your local supermarket.

Variation

Play around with different flavours in this breakfast biscuit. Try a different kind of extract, such as vanilla or almond. Try different nuts, too, such as pistachios, walnuts, or hazelnuts.

19

Fresco e delizioso
(Fresh and delicious)

For hundreds of years in Italy, markets were one of the main places where people met, gathered, and shared news. That is still true today. Customers often shop daily, stopping at separate stalls to buy cheese, meat, fruits, vegetables, and herbs. Italians keep their recipes simple to bring out the most flavour from these fresh ingredients.

Antipasti

In Italy, antipasti are served before a meal for a special occasion. This platter can be a colourful display to showcase the meats, cheeses, and marinated vegetables of Italy. Serve it with some crusty bread or grissini. Grissini are breadsticks invented in Turin in the 1600s.

Ingredients

1 bag of spring mixed greens (including rocket and radicchio)	Various jars of marinated vegetables, such as aubergine, artichoke hearts, roasted red peppers, pepperoncini, and black and green olives	Olive oil
100 g each prosciutto, capocolla, and mortadella		Balsamic vinegar
225 g each provolone, fresh mozzarella, and Parmesan		Italian bread or grissini

Tools

Large platter
Knife
Chopping board

Steps

1. Cover the platter with the greens.

2. Roll the individual slices of cured meats. Cut the cheese into slices or bite-size pieces. Arrange the meat and cheese on top of the lettuce.

3. Fill in open areas with the various marinated vegetables.

4. Lightly drizzle olive oil and balsamic vinegar over the platter.

5. Serve with slices of bread or grissini.

Makes about 8 to 10 appetizer servings
Time: About 20 to 30 minutes

Panzanella salad

This salad is a popular side dish in Tuscany, a region in the middle of Italy that includes the city of Florence. When bread sits out in the open air, it may become dry and crunchy. Instead of wasting this stale bread, Italians combine it with fresh herbs and vegetables to make a colourful salad.

Ingredients

Stale Italian bread (about 120 g), cut into cubes

2 large tomatoes, chopped

1 cucumber, peeled and chopped

½ small red onion, thinly sliced

1 sprig basil, torn into small pieces

5 tablespoons olive oil

Salt and pepper, to taste

Tools

Kitchen scales

Measuring spoons

Bowls

Knife

Chopping board

Spoon

Cling film

Steps

1. In a bowl, combine the tomatoes, cucumber, onion, basil, olive oil, and salt and pepper.

2. In another bowl, place about half of the bread cubes. Spoon half of the tomato mixture over the bread. Place the rest of the bread into the bowl, and spoon over the rest of the tomato mixture. By making layers, the juices will soak better into all the bread pieces.

3. Cover with cling film. Allow to sit at room temperature (not the refrigerator) for a few hours for the flavours to blend together.

4. Stir well before serving. Add salt and pepper to taste.

Quick tip

Don't put tomatoes in the refrigerator. They taste best when left at room temperature. In the fridge, they will turn soft and grainy and lose their fresh flavour.

Makes 4 to 6 servings
Time: About 15 minutes (plus a few hours for flavours to combine)

 airy free

 egetarian

23

Panino di Parma

A *panino* is an Italian sandwich. This panino combines the flavours of the city of Parma, home to prosciutto ham and Parmesan cheese. These ingredients, joined by rocket and balsamic vinegar, create an interesting play of sweet and salty in your mouth.

Ingredients

Focaccia bread

225 g thinly-sliced prosciutto

50 g Parmesan cheese

1 large handful rocket

1 to 2 tablespoons balsamic vinegar

Tools

Kitchen scales

Knife

Chopping board

Vegetable peeler

Bowl

Measuring spoons

Salad tongs

Steps

1. Slice the focaccia bread open to make the top and bottom for the sandwich.

2. Lay on a few slices of prosciutto.

3. With a vegetable peeler, thinly shave pieces of cheese and place them on the prosciutto.

4. In a bowl, toss the rocket with the balsamic vinegar. Place the dressed rocket onto the sandwich.

5. Top with the other half of the focaccia and serve.

VARIATION

Focaccia is a flat Italian bread, similar to pizza crust. But any crusty Italian bread will work well for this recipe. You can buy bread as a loaf and slice it yourself. Or look for ciabatta rolls to make individual sandwiches.

Makes 4 sandwiches
Time: About 10 minutes

25

Margherita pizza

Naples is considered the home of pizza. In Naples, pizza is made in traditional wood-burning ovens. One of the most famous creations to come from Naples is the margherita pizza. In 1889, the city welcomed Queen Margherita and her husband King Umberto I with a pizza covered with the colours of the Italian flag – red, white, and green.

Ingredients

Refrigerated pizza dough

Flour

Olive oil

1 (400-g) tin chopped tomatoes, drained

1 ball fresh mozzarella

A few sprigs of fresh basil

Salt and pepper, to taste

Tools

Rolling pin

Baking tray

Pastry brush

Knife

Chopping board

Steps

1. Preheat oven to 220°C.

2. Sprinkle flour on your chopping board or work surface. Roll out the dough into a rectangular shape. Transfer to a baking tray brushed with olive oil.

3. Cover the dough with the chopped tomatoes. Slice the mozzarella very thinly, and place all over the tomatoes. Season with salt and pepper.

4. Bake for about 10 minutes. Take out the baking tray, and sprinkle the basil on top of the pizza. Drizzle pizza with olive oil.

5. Return the pizza to the oven and cook for another 10 to 15 minutes, until the crust is browned around the edges and the cheese is lightly browned.

VARIATION

Instead of canned tomatoes, you can use fresh tomatoes for this recipe, too. Slice the tomatoes very thinly, and remove the seeds. This will keep the pizza from getting too soggy.

Makes 4 servings
Time: 15 minutes prep,
20 to 25 minutes to bake

Vegetarian

Basta pasta! (Enough pasta!)

Italians eat a lot of pasta. There are countless types of pasta to choose from. Some pasta, such as ravioli or tortellini, is filled with meat or cheese. Capellini are long, thin strands, penne are pointed tubes, and farfalle are shaped like bow ties. Use a smooth, long pasta for lighter sauces. Use pasta with grooves or holes to hold chunkier sauces. And remember to say *basta* (enough) before you feel stuffed!

Gorgonzola gnocchi

Gorgonzola is made from the milk of cows that are raised in Piedmont and Lombardy, two regions in northern Italy. The blue veins running through the cheese are actually mould, which gives the cheese a tangy flavour. Gnocchi are little dumplings made from potatoes and boiled like pasta.

Ingredients

100 g Gorgonzola cheese
120 ml double cream
120 ml skimmed milk

2 (500-g) packets potato gnocchi
Fresh parsley for garnish
Salt and pepper, to taste

Tools

Kitchen scales
Measuring jug
Saucepan
Spoon
Stockpot
Colander

Steps

1. In a saucepan, bring the milk and cream to a simmer over medium heat.

2. Turn down the heat to medium-low. Add the Gorgonzola and cook for about 5 minutes, stirring frequently, until the cheese melts and the sauce thickens slightly. Season with salt and pepper.

3. Meanwhile, cook the gnocchi in the stockpot according to packet directions. Drain in a colander.

4. Toss the sauce with the cooked gnocchi. Garnish with fresh parsley.

**Makes 4 to 6 servings
Time: About 15 minutes**

 Vegetarian

VARIATION

Look for gluten-free gnocchi in speciality shops if you want to avoid wheat flour.

Pasta with pesto

This basil-based sauce is Genoa's best-known dish. Long ago, people made pesto by mashing the ingredients together with a mortar and pestle. But it is much faster and easier with a blender. You can serve pesto as a pasta sauce, add it to soup, or even spread it on pizza or a sandwich.

Ingredients

3 or 4 handfuls of
    basil leaves
30 g pine nuts
1 large clove garlic, minced
4 tablespoons olive oil
Salt and pepper, to taste
30 g Parmesan cheese,
    grated
450 g dry spaghetti

Tools

Kitchen scales
Measuring spoons
Knife
Chopping board
Food processor or blender
Cheese grater
Bowl
Spoon
Stockpot
Colander

Steps

1. Wash and dry the basil leaves well.

2. Combine the basil, nuts, garlic, olive oil, and salt and pepper in a food processor to create a paste.

3. Transfer the paste to a bowl. Add the cheese and stir to combine.

4. Meanwhile, cook the pasta in the stockpot according to packet directions. Drain in a colander.

5. Toss the pesto with the pasta and serve.

Makes 4 to 6 servings
Time: About 20 minutes prep

VARIATION

Pine nuts are actually seeds. They come from cones of a stone pine tree. But if you can't find pine nuts, you could use walnuts to make pesto as well.

Ncontains**uts**   **V**egetarian

Tagliatelle with bolognese sauce

Bologna is known for this long-simmering meaty sauce served over tagliatelle, long, flat ribbons of pasta, also invented in this city. Since the sauce is so heavy, it needs pasta equal to the task of holding all this weight and flavour. If you can't find tagliatelle, you could use rigatoni (a short, wide tube) or cavatappi (thick corkscrews).

Ingredients

100 g diced pancetta
2 tablespoons olive oil
1 small onion, diced
2 stalks celery, diced
2 carrots, diced
2 cloves garlic, minced
450 g minced beef

Salt and pepper, to taste
120 ml beef stock
1 (400-g) tin chopped tomatoes
Water
240 ml milk
450 g dry pasta
Parmesan cheese

Tools

Kitchen scales
Measuring jug and spoons
Knife
Chopping board
2 stockpots
Spoon
Cheese grater

Steps

1. Place the diced pancetta in a stockpot with the olive oil. Cook for about 8 minutes on medium-high, stirring occasionally to brown all over. Add the diced onion, celery, carrots, and garlic. Cook for about 5 to 7 minutes more until the vegetables soften.

2. Add the beef and salt and pepper. Brown the beef for about 10 minutes.

3. Add the stock and chopped tomatoes (with juices) to deglaze the pan. Heat for around 2 to 3 minutes as the liquids evaporate. Scrape up any brown bits that have stuck to the pan and mix into the sauce.

4. Add the milk and bring to a simmer. Turn the heat down, and let the sauce simmer, half covered, for about 2 to 4 hours, stirring occasionally. Add water a little bit at a time as the liquids evaporate, to keep the sauce from drying out.

5. Meanwhile, cook the pasta according to packet directions. Drain and return to the pot.

6. Add the sauce and toss to combine. Serve with freshly grated Parmesan cheese.

Quick tip

Try to dice the onion, carrot, and celery into pieces all about the same size. That way they will all take about the same amount of time to cook.

Makes 6 servings
Time: 45 minutes prep,
  2 to 4 hours to simmer

Quant'è buono!
(How good it is!)

Many Italian dishes are cooked on the hob, filling the air with delicious Italian smells that invite others to the kitchen. Eating together has always been an important part of Italian culture. Family and friends enjoy each other's company while eating meals together.

Scampi

Scampi means prawns, a type of crustacean. You can also use large prawns for this recipe. Serve this dish over cooked pasta, or just soak up the lemony juices with some crusty Italian bread.

Ingredients

- 450 g raw large prawns, shelled and deveined
- 2 tablespoons olive oil
- 2 tablespoons butter
- 2 large cloves garlic, minced
- 120 ml vegetable stock
- 1 tablespoon dried parsley
- ½ teaspoon red chilli flakes
- Salt and pepper, to taste
- 1 tablespoon lemon juice

Tools

- Kitchen scales
- Chopping board
- Knife
- Measuring jug and spoons
- Frying pan
- Spoon
- Spatula

Steps

1. Heat the oil and the butter in a frying pan on medium high until the butter melts. Add the garlic and cook for about 1 minute.

2. Add the prawns, stock, parsley, red chilli flakes, salt, and pepper. Sauté the prawns for about 2 minutes on one side. Then flip them over to cook on the other side for about 1 minute more, until the prawns are pink and cooked through, and some of the liquid has evaporated.

3. Top with the lemon juice. Serve with pasta or bread.

Quick tip

Watch over your prawns the whole time they cook. Prawns cook very quickly. If you cook them for too long, they will have a rubbery texture.

Makes 4 servings
Time: About 10 minutes

Pasta e fagioli

Pasta and bean soup is one of the most common Italian soups. Different households in Italy make their own versions of this dish using different beans, pastas, and herbs. It is a hearty soup that is great for a cold day.

Ingredients

100 g diced pancetta
2 tablespoons olive oil
1 small onion, diced
2 cloves garlic, minced
1 bay leaf
½ teaspoon dried thyme
½ teaspoon dried rosemary
900 ml chicken stock

1 (400-g) tin chopped tomatoes
2 (400-g) tins cannellini beans, drained and rinsed
100 g dried ditalini pasta
Salt and pepper, to taste
Parmesan cheese, to finish

Tools

Kitchen scales
Knife
Chopping board
Measuring jug and spoons
Stockpot
Spoon
Potato masher or fork
Bowls
Grater

Steps

1. Place the diced pancetta in a stockpot with the olive oil, onion, garlic, bay leaf, thyme, and rosemary. Cook on medium to medium-high heat for about 10 minutes until the onions soften and the pancetta is browned.

2. Add the chicken stock, chopped tomatoes (with the liquid), and one can of beans.

3. Mash the other can of beans with a potato masher or back of a fork, then add to the soup.

4. Cover and bring to the boil. Turn the heat down and simmer for about 15 minutes. Add the pasta. Turn the heat up to medium and let it simmer in the soup for about 10 to 15 minutes, or until al dente.

5. Remove the bay leaf. Season with salt and pepper. Serve in bowls, with freshly grated Parmesan cheese.

Quick tip

Dry herbs are easy to have on hand to use when you need them. But if you want to season your soup like a true Italian, you may want to use fresh herbs. You can use fresh herbs more generously than dried herbs. A general rule is to use about 3 times more of a fresh herb than a dried one.

Dairy free
(without the Parmesan)

Makes 6 dinner-size servings
Time: About 50 minutes

Veal scaloppine with lemon sauce

Italy is known for its veal, the tender meat from calves, especially in the region of Lombardy. In Lombardy, this dish might be served with the creamy rice dish, risotto. Risotto takes patience, as you slowly stir stock into Arborio rice. If you'd rather make a meal faster, you can serve it with pasta or Italian bread instead.

Ingredients

450 g veal scaloppine cutlets

Flour

Salt and pepper, to taste

2 tablespoons olive oil

80 ml chicken stock

Juice of 1 lemon

1 tablespoon butter

Tools

Kitchen scales

Measuring jug
    and spoons

Plate

Frying pan

Spatula

Dish and kitchen foil

Spoon

Steps

1. Sprinkle some flour on a plate, and coat each piece of veal in the flour. Season with salt and pepper.

2. Heat the olive oil in the frying pan. Place the veal pieces into the pan. Do not overcrowd them.

3. Cook for about 2 minutes on one side until lightly browned. Flip over and cook for about 2 minutes on the other side until no longer pink. Remove from the pan and set aside in a dish covered with foil to keep warm.

4. Add the stock, lemon juice, and butter to the pan. Bring to the boil, and cook for about 1 minute, stirring constantly.

5. Put each portion of veal on a plate and pour sauce over it. Serve with pasta, bread, or risotto.

VARIATIONS

Some people prefer not to eat veal. You can make this dish with chicken instead. You may be able to find chicken prepared for scaloppine. If not, place your chicken cutlets between two pieces of cling film and use a kitchen mallet to pound them thin.

Makes 4 servings
Time: 20 to 25 minutes

La dolce vita (The sweet life)

Living in Italy is sometimes described as "the sweet life". That might be because Italians often take the time to enjoy each moment. Strolling through city squares or sitting outside a café for a treat is a common way to spend one's time.

Most Italian meals don't include dessert – more often an Italian might just have some dried fruit, nuts, or fresh fruit. *Dolci* (sweets) are often served for special occasions and help Italians truly enjoy a sweet life!

Panna cotta

Panna cotta means "cooked cream". This traditional dessert is often served with fresh fruit or a sauce on top. You can unmould it upside down onto a plate, or just eat it out of the bowl.

Ingredients

240 ml whole milk

1 tablespoon unflavoured gelatin

500 ml double cream

100 g sugar

Fresh raspberries and blueberries (or any fresh berries)

Tools

Kitchen scales

2 saucepans

Spoon

Whisk

Measuring jug and spoons

6 small bowls or ramekins

Baking tray with high sides

Warm water

Plates

Steps

1. In a medium saucepan, combine the milk and gelatin. Warm on medium-low heat and stir for about 4 to 5 minutes until the gelatin dissolves. Remove from the heat and set aside.

2. Add the cream and the sugar to another saucepan. Bring just to the boil over medium-high heat, stirring constantly with a whisk for about 8 to 10 minutes, until the sugar is completely dissolved. Remove from the heat.

3. Pour the cream and sugar mixture into the saucepan with the milk and gelatin mixture. Stir to combine.

4. Transfer the mixture into a measuring jug. Use the jug to pour the mixture into six small bowls or ramekins.

5. Allow to cool to room temperature. Then place in the refrigerator for 4 to 6 hours to set.

6. To unmould the panna cotta, set the bowl in a baking tray with some warm water to help loosen it. Then turn the bowl upside down over the serving plate. Jiggle it until it falls onto the plate.

7. Serve the panna cotta with fresh berries on top.

luten free   **V**egetarian
(with vegetarian gelatin)

Makes 6 servings
Time: 15 to 20 minutes to prep and cook, 4 to 6 hours to set

Tartufo

This ice cream "truffle" is made to look like a luxurious black mushroom grown in Umbria that is sniffed out by specially trained dogs. But this tartufo doesn't taste like a mushroom! It is coated in chocolate and has a surprise cherry in the centre.

Ingredients

Chocolate ice cream
12 maraschino cherries
300 g dark chocolate chips
2 tablespoons vegetable oil

Tools

Kitchen scales
Ice cream scoop
Baking tray
Greaseproof paper
Microwave-safe bowl
Spoons
Cooling rack
Muffin tray
Cupcake cases

Steps

1. Leave the ice cream out of the freezer until slightly soft. Scoop out a ball of ice cream, and hold it in your hand. Push a cherry into the centre, and reform into a ball.

2. Place the ice cream ball onto a baking tray covered with greaseproof paper. Repeat to make 11 more chocolate balls. Work quickly, because the ice cream will melt.

3. Place the baking tray into the freezer. Allow the ice cream balls to freeze solid again, around 1 hour. (You can also work in batches, making four at a time so they don't melt as you work.)

4. In a microwave-safe bowl, combine the chocolate chips and the vegetable oil. Microwave on high for 30 seconds. Stir. Microwave for another 30 seconds. Stir until the chocolate is smooth and runny.

5. Take the ice cream balls out of the freezer. Place on a cooling rack with a piece of greaseproof paper underneath. Spoon the chocolate mixture over each ice cream ball to coat the top and sides completely.

6. Lift each ice cream ball with a spoon, and place in a cupcake case in a muffin tray. Place back in the freezer for another hour or more until completely hardened again.

7. Serve with a few more cherries.

Makes 6 servings
Time: About 30 minutes prep,
        2 hours to freeze

luten
free
egetarian

VARiATiON

Any kind of ice cream works for this dessert. Use your favourite! While the melted chocolate is still soft, you can sprinkle it with chocolate chips or chocolate sprinkles.

Glossary

Tools

chopping board flat work surface that protects worktops from knife marks when cutting food

colander bowl-shaped tool with holes for draining liquid from foods

frying pan pan with a long handle and low sides for use on the hob

greaseproof paper paper used for baking that keeps food from sticking to the baking tray

kitchen scales device used to measure the weight of food ingredients

measuring jug and spoons A measuring jug is marked with lines along the side to measure liquids. Measuring spoons come in different sizes to help you measure accurate amounts.

platter large dish meant for serving food

ramekin individual serving-size baking dish

saucepan pan with a long handle, lid, and high sides for use on the hob

spatula type of utensil with a flat end. Some spatulas are used for mixing, spreading, and scraping the sides of pots and bowls. Others are used for flipping food or removing it from the pan.

stockpot large, round metal pot with handles on each side and a lid for use on the hob

whisk tool used to break down ingredients and bring air into a mixture

Terms

al dente	cook until food is soft, but still has some firmness
brine	liquid made from water and salt used to preserve food
cream	mix foods until smooth
deglaze	add a liquid to a pan to dissolve bits of food stuck on the bottom
dice	cut into small pieces (smaller than chopping, but bigger than mincing)
drizzle	pour a liquid lightly over food
evaporate	heat so that liquid changes to vapour
marinate	soak in a liquid and spices to add flavour
mince	cut into very fine pieces
sauté	cook in a pan with a little fat, such as oil or butter
serrated	having an uneven, jagged edge for cutting
simmer	cook over low heat so that the liquid bubbles gently, but does not boil
to taste	amount that tastes best to you
whisk	beat quickly with a whisk to break down ingredients and bring air into a mixture

Find out more

Books

Italy (Been There!), Annabel Savery (Franklin Watts, 2011)

Italy (Countries Around the World), Claire Throp (Raintree, 2012)

Italy (Countries in Our World), Ann Weil (Franklin Watts, 2012)

Italy (Food and Celebrations), Sylvia Goulding (Wayland, 2008)

Italy (Looking at Countries), Jillian Powell (Franklin Watts, 2011)

DVDs

Rick Stein's Mediterranean Escapes (BBC DVD), Rick Stein (2entertain, 2009)

Rotten Romans (Horrible Histories), Scholastic (Delta Music GMbH, 2005)

Websites

Food Standards Agency
www.food.gov.uk/multimedia/pdfs/kitchen-check-yppack.pdf
Play these fun puzzles to help you stay safe in the kitchen.

The eatwell plate
food.gov.uk/scotland/scotnut/eatwellplate/#.UevoDNKsiSo
This site describes a healthy, balanced way to get all the
nutrients you need in the right proportions.

BBC: Primary History: Romans
www.bbc.co.uk/schools/primaryhistory/romans
Explore interactive pages full of facts, photos, and videos.

National Geographic Kids: Italy
kids.nationalgeographic.com/kids/places/find/italy
View videos, look at maps, and read lots of information
on this interactive site.

Time for Kids: Italy
www.timeforkids.com/destination/italy
Visit this site to see lots of pictures, learn some Italian,
and follow an Italian girl through her day.

Further research

If this book gave you a taste for Italian food, there are
many more Italian cookbooks you could look at. You
could also locate Italian restaurants or bakeries in your
own town or city to try a bite of authentic Italian dishes.

You may also be curious about Italy's history and culture.
Visit your local library and ask a librarian to help you
learn more. Or ask a parent to help you look up websites
for recipes, museums, or other information about Italy.

Index